Fighting Fire
Fire Trucks in Action

by Mari Schuh

Consulting Editor: Gail Saunders-Smith, PhD

Consultant: Keith S. Frangiamore, Vice President of Operations
Fire Safety Consultants Inc., Elgin, Illinois

Capstone
press

Mankato, Minnesota

Pebble Plus is published by Capstone Press,
151 Good Counsel Drive, P.O. Box 669, Mankato, Minnesota 56002.
www.capstonepress.com

072011   006231CGVMI

Library of Congress Cataloging-in-Publication Data
Schuh, Mari C., 1975–
    Fire trucks in action / by Mari Schuh.
    p. cm. — (Pebble plus. Fighting fire)
    Includes bibliographical references and index.
    Summary: "In simple text and photos, presents fire trucks and what they are used for" — Provided by publisher.
    ISBN-13: 978-1-4296-1725-3 (hardcover)
    ISBN-10: 1-4296-1725-X (hardcover)
    1. Fire engines — Juvenile literature. I. Title. II. Series
TH9372.S38 2009
628.9'259 — dc22   2008026956

Editorial Credits
Sarah L. Schuette, editor; Tracy Davies, designer; Marcy Morin, photo shoot scheduler

Photo Credits
Capstone Press/Karon Dubke, all

Note to Parents and Teachers

The Fighting Fire set supports national science standards related to science, technology, and
society. This book describes and illustrates fire trucks in action. The images support early
readers in understanding the text. The repetition of words and phrases helps early readers
learn new words. This book also introduces early readers to subject-specific vocabulary words,
which are defined in the Glossary section. Early readers may need assistance to read some
words and to use the Table of Contents, Glossary, Read More, Internet Sites, and Index
sections of the book.

Table of Contents

Fire Trucks

Firefighters use fire trucks
to get to fires.
Lights and sirens let people
know there's an emergency.

Fire trucks carry long hoses.

The strong hoses spray

water on fires.

Types of Trucks

Fire engines lead the way when the fire alarm rings. Firefighters ride in the back of fire engines.

Pumper trucks carry
their own water.
They carry hoses to get
more water from hydrants.

Ladder trucks have
very long ladders.
The ladders reach high
to save people
in tall buildings.

Tools

Fire trucks carry

axes and saws.

Firefighters use the tools

to let smoke

out of buildings.

Some fire trucks carry
medical supplies.
They hold first-aid kits,
backboards, and air tanks.

Fire trucks hold tools
to rescue people.
The big tools can
cut open smashed cars.

Always Ready

Fire trucks are always ready
for the next fire.

Glossary

axe — a sharp tool used to fight fires; an axe has a long handle and a sharp metal end.

depend — to need and trust something or someone

hydrant — a large outdoor pipe connected to a water supply

siren — an object that makes a very loud sound as a warning

supplies — items that are needed often; fire trucks hold supplies such as first-aid kits, face masks, and air tanks.

Read More

Lindeen, Mary. *Fire Trucks*. Mighty Machines. Minneapolis: Bellwether Media, 2007.

Randolph, Joanne. *Fire Trucks*. To the Rescue! New York: PowerKids Press, 2008.

Roberts, Cynthia. *Fire Trucks*. Machines at Work. Chanhassen, Minn.: Child's World, 2007.

Internet Sites

FactHound offers a safe, fun way to find educator-approved Internet sites related to this book.

Here's what you do:

1. Visit *www.facthound.com*
2. Choose your grade level.
3. Begin your search.

This book's ID number is 9781429617253.

FactHound will fetch the best sites for you!

Index

Word Count: 132

Grade: 1

Early-Intervention Level: 18